GERALD FORD

The Presidents of the United States

George Washington
1789–1797

John Adams
1797–1801

Thomas Jefferson
1801–1809

James Madison
1809–1817

James Monroe
1817–1825

John Quincy Adams
1825–1829

Andrew Jackson
1829–1837

Martin Van Buren
1837–1841

William Henry Harrison
1841

John Tyler
1841–1845

James Polk
1845–1849

Zachary Taylor
1849–1850

Millard Fillmore
1850–1853

Franklin Pierce
1853–1857

James Buchanan
1857–1861

Abraham Lincoln
1861–1865

Andrew Johnson
1865–1869

Ulysses S. Grant
1869–1877

Rutherford B. Hayes
1877–1881

James Garfield
1881

Chester Arthur
1881–1885

Grover Cleveland
1885–1889

Benjamin Harrison
1889–1893

Grover Cleveland
1893–1897

William McKinley
1897–1901

Theodore Roosevelt
1901–1909

William H. Taft
1909–1913

Woodrow Wilson
1913–1921

Warren Harding
1921–1923

Calvin Coolidge
1923–1929

Herbert Hoover
1929–1933

Franklin D. Roosevelt
1933–1945

Harry Truman
1945–1953

Dwight Eisenhower
1953–1961

John F. Kennedy
1961–1963

Lyndon B. Johnson
1963–1969

Richard Nixon
1969–1974

Gerald Ford
1974–1977

Jimmy Carter
1977–1981

Ronald Reagan
1981–1989

George H. W. Bush
1989–1993

William J. Clinton
1993–2001

George W. Bush
2001–2009

Barack Obama
2009–

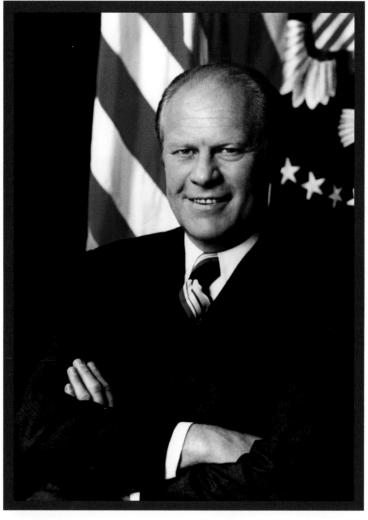

GERALD FORD
WIL MARA

 Marshall Cavendish
Benchmark
New York

Marshall Cavendish Benchmark
99 White Plains Road
Tarrytown, NY 10591-5502
www.marshallcavendish.us

All Internet addresses were correct at the time of printing.

Library of Congress Cataloging-in-Publication Data

Mara, Wil.
Gerald Ford / by Wil Mara.
p. cm. — (Presidents and their times)
Summary: "Provides comprehensive information on President Gerald Ford and places him
within his historical and cultural context. Also explored are the formative events of his times
and how he responded."—Provided by publisher.
Includes bibliographical references and index.
ISBN 978-0-7614-3629-4
1. Ford, Gerald R., 1913–2006—Juvenile literature. 2. Presidents—United States—Biography—Juvenile
literature. 3. United States—Politics and government—1974–1977—Juvenile literature. I. Title.
E866.M37 2009
973.925092—dc22
[B]
2008028412

Editor: Christine Florie
Publisher: Michelle Bisson
Art Director: Anahid Hamparian
Series Designer: Alex Ferrari

Photo research by Connie Gardner

Cover photo by Roger L. Wollenberg/Pool/epa/Corbis

The photographs in this book are used by permission and through the courtesy of: *Corbis:* Bettmann, 3,
9, 10, 13, 15, 16, 22, 25, 42, 44, 49, 60, 66, 68, 76, 78, 83, 84, 95, 96 (L), 97 (L), Hulton Deutsch, 27,
Arnie Sachs, 56, Owen Franken, 65, 86; Wally McNamee, 90; *The Image Works:* Snark Archives c
Photo12, 11; Mary Evans Picture Library, 21; Topham, 28, Charles Gatewood, 47; Mark Godfrey, 80;
AP Photo: 31, 32, 36, 38, 39, 41, 54, 58, 96 (R); *The Granger Collection:* 24; *Getty Images:* Time and
Life Pictures, 6, 69, 73; Getty, 63; CBS Photo Archive, 88; Wireimage, 91; AFP, 93, 97 (R).

Printed in Malaysia
1 3 5 6 4 2

CONTENTS

Vice President Gerald Ford was sworn in as the nation's thirty-eighth president the same day that President Richard Nixon resigned from the presidency.

MICHIGAN BOY

The date was August 9, 1974, a Friday. The mood in the East Room of the White House, with its sparkling chandeliers and thick gold curtains, was a peculiar mix of sadness and optimism.

The sadness came from the gloomy events that transpired earlier in the day. Richard M. Nixon delivered a gut-wrenching speech. He was the fallen president, a man so complex and extreme that even those who had worked closely with him for decades felt they never saw the real person behind the public façade. Some of the men who worked for him took part in a burglary, and Nixon claimed he didn't know anything about it. But it turned out he *did* know about it—he had lied, and then he got caught. Before he could be stripped of the presidency, he resigned. In America, even the president of the United States wasn't above the law. So Nixon would put on a brave face this day, walk out of the White House for the last time, and board a helicopter that would take him away from professional politics forever. Disgrace would go with him, and history would pass a heavy judgment.

But there was also hope, because Nixon's vice president would take over. His name was Gerald Ford, and he was known as a man of integrity and honesty. He had never campaigned for the presidency, never desired it, but perhaps that was his greatest asset.

Shortly after noon, Ford stepped onto the stage, placed his left hand on the Bible, and swore before God and his fellow countrymen that he would "faithfully execute the office of the

President of the United States." It was a colossal task, to be sure—the nation was still in the throes of the Vietnam War, jobs were vanishing by the thousands, the cost of everything from food to gasoline was rising to staggering new highs, and public trust in government was all but gone. Indeed, there was a great deal of work to be done.

After Ford finished the oath, he gave a speech, expressing his faith in the American people and the American way of life. He asked for prayers and good wishes. He promised to do everything in his power to make things better. And he made an announcement that many had been waiting to hear, "My fellow Americans, our long national nightmare is over."

And with that, Ford began his presidency.

EARLY YEARS

Gerald Rudolph Ford Jr. was born in Omaha, Nebraska, shortly after midnight on July 14, 1913. His name at birth was Leslie Lynch King Jr. His father, Leslie Sr., came from a wealthy banking family and was a wool trader. His mother, Dorothy, was a housewife. The couple had met in college, where Dorothy was impressed by Leslie's well-to-do mannerisms and affluence. But her image of the man changed soon after their wedding when she discovered that he not only had a terrible temper, but also a tendency toward violence. On their honeymoon, he beat her savagely after wrongfully accusing her of flirting with another man.

She dealt with the abuse for a while, but ran out of patience shortly after their son was born and her husband threatened to kill both of them with a knife. In an era when women rarely left their husbands no matter how harsh the circumstances, Dorothy made the brave decision to gather up her child and flee the abusive relationship, seeking happier pas-

tures at her parents' home in Grand Rapids, Michigan.

There, Dorothy began attending services at a local Episcopal church where she met a kindhearted and hardworking twenty-five-year-old salesman named Gerald Rudolf Ford. He took a liking to Dorothy's young son. Dorothy and Gerald were married in February of 1917, and Gerald accepted young Leslie as his own child. The couple began calling him Gerald Rudolf Ford Jr., a name that he used for the rest of his life though he was never officially adopted by his stepfather (although, when he had it legally changed in December of 1935, he altered the spelling of Rudolf to Rudolph). Gerald Sr. and Dorothy would eventually have three more

Gerald Ford was Dorothy Gardner's first child.

After leaving an abusive relationship, Ford's mother married the good-natured Gerald Rudolf Ford.

sons together, giving young Jerry three half brothers. The future president's biological father would also have more children from a second marriage, giving him another half brother and two half sisters.

The Great War

During Gerald's early childhood, far away from the peace and quiet of Grand Rapids, a bloody conflict was raging. World War I, also known as The Great War, began in June of 1914 following the assassination of Austria–Hungary's Archduke Franz Ferdinand. Germany was also involved because they formed a union with Austria–Hungary known as the Central powers. Their opponents at the start of the war, called the Allied powers, were the nations of Russia, France, and Great Britain. In the weeks and months that followed, other countries in the region joined one side or the other.

America's policy for the first few years of the war was to remain neutral, but President Woodrow Wilson had a feeling he wouldn't be able to maintain that neutrality for long. In early 1917 he learned that Germany had asked Mexico to fight with them against America, pushing Wilson to act. On April 6, 1917, the United States officially became a part of the Allied effort.

American troops march through the streets of Saint Nazaire, France, in support of the Allied effort during World War I.

American troops began landing in Europe a few months later, lending manpower, equipment, and money to the Allied forces. Germany and its partners surrendered shortly thereafter. World War I officially ended on November 11, 1918.

YOUNG JERRY FORD AND THE GREAT DEPRESSION

In elementary and high school, Jerry was a good, although not exceptional, student. He was well liked by his classmates, with a reputation as an honest and cheerful individual. Growing up in a town that had beautiful lakes and forests, and with a family who loved outdoor activities, he was all but destined to become a Boy Scout. He joined Troop 15 on December 17, 1924. He was

EAGLE SCOUT PRESIDENT

Just three years after joining the Scouts, Ford would earn twenty-six merit badges and become an Eagle Scout, the highest rank a Scout can achieve—and he would be the only U.S. president ever to do so. In the White House years, Ford wrote the following in a letter to the Scouts:

The three great principles which Scouting encourages—self-discipline, teamwork, and moral and patriotic values—are the building blocks of character. By working for these principles, those who belong to and support the Boy Scouts of America add greatly to the vitality of our society and to the future well-being of its people.

Gerald Ford was a typical boy during his early years in Grand Rapids, Michigan.

also a superb athlete with a particular aptitude for football. Playing both center (offense) and linebacker (defense), he led his high school to a state championship during his senior year, in 1930. His talents caught the attention of several colleges, including the prestigious Harvard and Northwestern universities. Ford chose, however, to stay close to home and attend the University of Michigan in Ann Arbor, where he also got a job washing dishes to help pay for his expenses.

The fact that Ford was able to find a job at all was something of a lucky break, as America was struggling with the most difficult economic downturn it may ever know—a period called the Great Depression. The seeds of the Depression had been planted following World War I.

In America the 1920s began with the demand for all sorts of new and interesting products such as cars, radios, and kitchen appliances. And there was a new way to afford these things, too—on **credit**. The problem was that many spent more than they could cover later on. By the end of the 1920s, the financial system of America was nearing a breaking point. On Thursday, October 24, 1929—a date known as Black Thursday—and climaxing on Tuesday, October 29, the value of American stocks fell about 80 percent. As a result, millions of people lost millions of dollars. Year after year, the **economy** continued to sink. By 1933 the unemployment rate hit a record high of 25 percent. That meant one person out of every four couldn't find a job.

Jerry Ford's family didn't end up living in the streets, but they were still adversely affected by the Great Depression. Gerald Sr. and Dorothy were forced to sell their large home in Grand Rapids in order to move into something smaller and more affordable.

Those affected by the Depression stand in line seeking shelter and a place to eat.

17

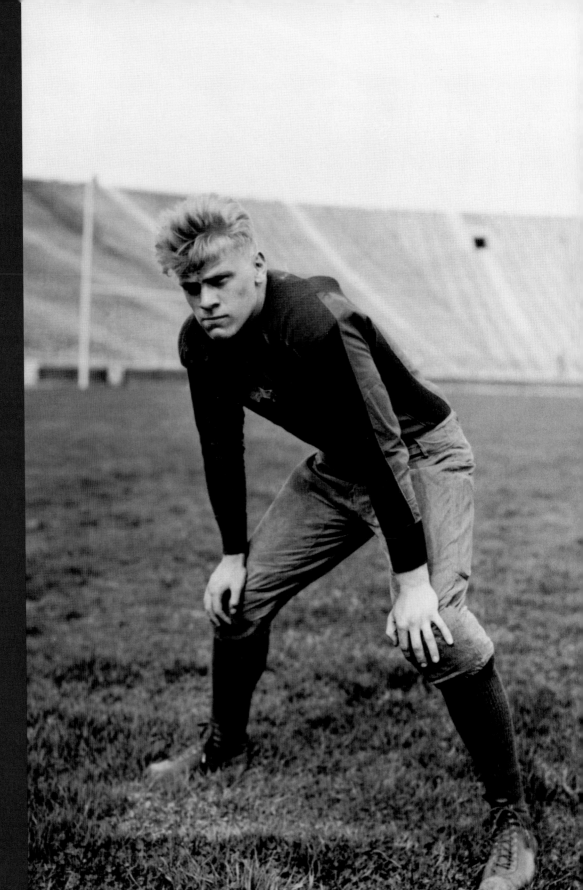

Ford attended
the University
of Michigan,
in Ann Arbor.
While there,
he played for
the school's
football team.

AN UNEASY MEETING

Ford met with his biological father in the spring of 1930 while working in a local restaurant in Grand Rapids. His father simply showed up one day, introduced himself, and invited his son to lunch. Jerry, sixteen, was hesitant at first, but finally agreed to go along. They talked about unimportant things because neither wanted to get too personal. Afterward, his father handed him some money. Jerry went home, told the entire story to his mother and stepfather, then went to his room and cried.

During his first two years at the University of Michigan, Jerry was unable to secure a starting spot on the school's football team, the Wolverines. They already had talented players in his two positions. But the future president, with his typical good nature, continued working on his skills and hoped for the best, securing a spot on the team in 1934. In spite of the Wolverines' dismal season that year, Ford became their most valuable player. Then he was given the chance to play against the National Football League's Chicago Bears in 1935 as a member of a collegiate all-star team. His performance was good enough to catch the attention of several NFL scouts. Both the Detroit Lions and the Green Bay Packers made him offers to play for their team. But Ford, after careful consideration, turned them both down— he wanted to go to law school.

From Lawyer to Soldier

*F*ord had several reasons for choosing law school over the NFL. He felt that a career in football wouldn't ultimately amount to much. Also, a career in professional sports usually only lasted a few years, and Ford was thinking farther ahead. Finally, he liked the idea that an attorney had the power to do some good in the world. He later said, "I thought my talents would be those of the mediator and counselor. As Abraham Lincoln once wrote: 'It is as a peacemaker that the lawyer has a superior opportunity.' That appealed to me."

Making the decision to go to law school was one thing, but getting there was another. The biggest hurdle was that he didn't have any money. America was slowly pulling itself out of the Great Depression, but the economy was far from stable. So Ford decided to set his sights on getting a job at a college that had a law program.

He tried first to secure a position as an assistant football coach at the University of Michigan, but they weren't hiring. The head coach, however, liked Ford and helped him find an assistant's position at Yale University in New Haven, Connecticut—one of the most respected schools in the nation. Ford interviewed with Yale's coach and was offered the job. It seemed like a tremendously lucky break—a paying job at a prestigious school that had a law program.

Unfortunately, the school directors felt that Ford's coaching duties would take up most of his time, so they denied him entry into Yale's law school that September. For the remainder of 1935 through the first half of 1937, Ford's participation at Yale was limited to coaching the football and boxing teams. While he may have enjoyed both positions on a personal level, he was still determined to stick to his plans of attending Yale's excellent law school.

He went back to the University of Michigan in the summer of 1937 and took several law classes, earning a B average and proving that he was a worthy student. Then he returned to Yale that autumn and was, at last, allowed to take a few classes. Yale's directors were still concerned that he would be unable to juggle such a busy schedule—football coach, boxing coach, and law student. But Ford managed to be successful at all three, and he was ultimately allowed to take law classes full-time. In the end, he would earn excellent grades and graduate in the top 25 percent of his class. In January of 1941 he returned to Michigan with his Yale degree and passed the **bar exam**.

Ford started a law firm in Grand Rapids, Michigan, with Phil Buchen, an old college friend from his University of Michigan days. Normally in those days a young lawyer would try to find a job with a well-established firm or a large business that maintained its own legal staff. But Ford, by his own words, said that, "Phil and I were impatient and ambitious; we decided to strike out on our own. As soon as we passed the bar, we formed the firm of Ford and Buchen and waited anxiously for clients to appear." Unfortunately, those all-important clients didn't appear right away, and the firm struggled at first with almost no money to support itself. Eventually, however, Ford and Buchen's reputation began to grow, and soon they were busier than they ever imagined.

WORLD WAR II

After World War I, Europe spent much of its time simply trying to recover. The hardships were greater for some countries than others—Germany, for example, barely had a foundation upon which to rebuild itself. The **Treaty of Versailles** left the once-proud nation with huge debts, no military, depleted resources, and the dismal burden of global humiliation.

Angered by their government's inability to improve the situation, the German people turned to a rising political leader who was giving voice to their frustrations—Adolf Hitler. At one time broke and homeless, Hitler had joined the **Nazi Party** and recognized the desperation of his fellow countrymen as a way of

THE MISUNDERSTOOD ARTIST

Adolf Hitler nearly became an artist instead of a cruel dictator. As a young man he showed some artistic promise and desperately wanted to attend the Academy of Fine Arts in Vienna. He sent samples of his work to the admissions department, but was turned down twice while struggling to eke out an existence in the beautiful Austrian capital city. Soon he was out of money, dispirited, and living in a homeless shelter. He also considered pursuing a career in architecture during this period, but ultimately went into politics instead.

Adolf Hitler and fellow Nazis salute at the Nuremberg Rally circa 1932.

elevating himself to power. In 1933 he became the nation's chancellor and outlawed all other political parties. Then he defied the Treaty of Versailles by rebuilding Germany's military forces. Meanwhile, he tried to reassure the world that he wasn't interested in war. "Germany needs peace and desires peace!" he insisted in a speech given in May of 1935.

Around the same time, Japan was looking to expand its own power in eastern Asia. Japan had fought on the side of the Allies in World War I and, as a result, had gained a great deal of land, resources, and political influence. But they wanted more, and they set their sights on weaker neighboring nations. In 1931 the Japanese military invaded and occupied nearby Manchuria (most of which lies within northeastern China), with the intent of ultimately conquering China in its entirety.

In 1939 Adolf Hitler decided to take similar action—wishing to expand the German empire, he invaded Poland in September of 1939. He also overtook the nations of Denmark, Norway, Belgium, Luxembourg, and the Netherlands in a span of just three months. France was next—and here Hitler had some help from Italy, under the dictatorship of his friend and ally Benito Mussolini. By 1941 Germany, Italy, and Japan had signed a pact to help fulfill their joint ambitions. These three nations, along with Bulgaria, Finland, Hungary, and Romania, eventually became known as the Axis powers, whereas those fighting against them (a group that would eventually constitute nearly fifty countries) would, just as in World War I, be called the Allied powers. And thus **World War II** would be

German troops ride through a Polish town after it was demolished from repeated bombings.

fought in two main **theaters**—the European theater, where Germany was looking to expand its empire, and the Pacific theater, where Japan was looking to do the same.

President Franklin Delano Roosevelt began selling war materials to Allied nations shortly after Hitler invaded Poland, but he wanted to keep America out of the actual fighting. By 1941, however, Japan had begun to view America as an enemy. Japan wanted to invade the nearby nations of Thailand and the Philippines. First, though, they had to cripple American naval forces stationed in nearby Pearl Harbor, in Hawaii. On December 7, 1941, more than 360 Japanese planes carried out a surprise bombing campaign on the Pearl Harbor base for almost two hours. In the end, more than 2,300 American soldiers and citizens were killed. Nine ships sank and more than twenty others were heavily damaged. America declared war on Japan the next day following President Roosevelt's speech to Congress in which he said, "I ask that the Congress declare that since the unprovoked and dastardly attack by Japan on Sunday, December 7, 1941, a state of war has existed between the United States and the Japanese Empire."

ENSIGN FORD

With America now involved in World War II, the patriotic Ford didn't want to sit in his law office all day—he wanted to be part of the fighting. He joined the navy on April 20, 1942, at the age of twenty-eight, and was given the rank of ensign. He was sent first for training at the Naval Academy in Annapolis, Maryland, then assigned to a flight school in North Carolina. Due to his extensive background in athletics, he was ordered to oversee the school's physical fitness program. This, however, wasn't what he had in mind when he decided to join the service. He wrote dozens of

Battleships in Pearl Harbor billow smoke after being bombed by the Japanese on December 7, 1941.

letters begging to be included in combat action, and his persist-ence eventually paid off—in the spring of 1943 he was assigned to the aircraft carrier USS *Monterey*. He would have two roles on the *Monterey*, the first being similar to what he'd done at the flight school—athletic director. The second job was as a gunnery officer, which meant he had to coordinate and direct the men who fired antiaircraft weapons.

Gerald Ford served in the U.S. military from 1942 to 1946.

His first taste of real combat action occurred in the Pacific Ocean the following November. The *Monterey* took part in attacks on Japanese forces in several island groups. Shortly after Christmas, Ford was given a new assignment—assistant navigator. This meant he would work with the head navigator to plan the ship's routes, determine its position at all times, and watch for obstacles along the way. This thrilled him, for he would now, truly, be in the center of the action.

A Shift in the Winds of War

By September 1942 Hitler's forces seemed to be moving into every sector of Europe. But then a series of failures marked the beginning of change. Hitler tried, for example, to conquer Great Britain through a series of relentless air strikes. But the plan didn't work—Britain had a new instrument called radar that forewarned of oncoming planes, and they were able to prepare for the attacks. Hitler's armies also tried to invade deeper into Soviet territory, but when the brutal Soviet winter arrived, the ill-equipped German forces in that region had to surrender. With the enemy's advances halted, the Allied powers began their own attacks.

They invaded Sicily in July of 1943 and moved into Italy the following September. In June of 1944, Allied forces landed in Normandy, France, and rid Europe of most Nazi occupation by the end of the year. In the Pacific theater, Allied forces focused their first major attacks on the island of Guadalcanal (part of the Solomon Islands). The fighting raged from August of 1942 until February of 1943, ending in a crucial Allied victory. American marines invaded the island of Saipan in June, Guam Island in July, and Peleliu Island in September. Then, in October, American navy vessels entered the Leyte Gulf for what would be the

American troops land in Normandy, France, on June 6, 1944, in an effort to defeat the Nazis in Europe.

last major sea battle in the Pacific theater. It spanned four days and ended in a crushing loss for the Japanese fleet. An Allied victory was close at hand.

The exhausted German military attempted one last offensive in December known as the Battle of the Bulge—but the Allies squelched it in less than two weeks. By April 1945 Russian troops had reached the German capital of Berlin. On April 30, hiding in his underground bunker while Russian troops were mere blocks away, Adolf Hitler committed suicide. One week later, on May 7, acting German commander Alfred Jodl signed an unconditional surrender.

In the Pacific, the Japanese decided to fight on. In spite of numerous Allied advances and gains, the Japanese hoped to make the battles so bloody and costly that the Allies would be willing to negotiate a peace settlement. Fearing this would cause hundreds of thousands of further deaths, U.S. president

The first atomic bomb was dropped on Hiroshima in 1945, causing massive destruction and thousands of deaths.

Harry S. Truman (who had been Roosevelt's vice president when Roosevelt died on April 12) decided to drop two recently developed atomic bombs on Japanese cities—one on Hiroshima (on August 6), the other on Nagasaki (on August 9)—resulting in tremendous devastation. As a result, Japan surrendered on September 12, ending World War II.

By this time, Ford's ship, the *Monterey*, had been ordered to port for some much-needed repairs, and Ford was reassigned to a naval training center in Illinois. He had already requested another combat assignment, but was denied since the end of the war was near. He remained at the training center for a few more months, then received his formal military discharge in February of 1946 with a final rank of lieutenant commander. It was time to go home.

MR. FORD GOES TO WASHINGTON

$\mathcal{R}$eturning home from the war, Ford intended to continue his career as a lawyer. The firm he had created with his friend, Phil Buchen, was no more—Buchen had gone to work for a larger and more prestigious firm, Butterfield, Keeney, and Amberg. Ford did briefly consider the possibility of restarting their old partnership, but he decided instead to join Buchen at his new firm in 1946.

Ford also began developing his interest in civic affairs. He joined several different local clubs and societies, feeling as though he could do some good for the Grand Rapids community. He also adopted a larger political view on America. Before the war, he considered himself a strict **isolationist**. He didn't believe America should get involved in issues concerning other nations; the country should focus on internal matters instead. After the war, however, his view shifted radically—he became an ardent **internationalist**, believing America, now a world power, was entwined in global politics whether it wanted to be or not. So the U.S. government needed to play a leading role in the issues of all nations. "My wartime experiences had given me an entirely new perspective," he said. Ford believed that the United States should put more time, energy, and funding into a stronger military defense, in light of the fact that World War II had also elevated the Soviet Union into a world power. Soviet government followed **communism** (the direct opposite of America's **capitalism**), so the Soviets could prove to be a threat to national interests in the not-too-distant future.

Between Ford's law practice and his community activities, his family began to worry that he had no social life—no friends, no free time, and no fun. His mother reminded him that he was in his mid-thirties and still didn't have a steady girlfriend. "You're 34 years old," she said one day. "When are you going to settle down?"

A female acquaintance of Ford's suggested a friend of hers named Betty Warren. Ford had met Warren before, but he never got to know her very well. Nevertheless, he remembered her as

It was during the mid-1940s that Gerald Ford met and began dating his future wife, Betty Warren.

affable and attractive. There was one snag, however—Betty Warren was married to someone else. She had been in an unhappy marriage for five years, and she was in the process of getting a divorce when Ford called. She told him that she didn't feel it was appropriate to date until the divorce was final. "I'm in the process of getting a divorce, and you're a lawyer, you ought to know better," she said. But Ford was persistent, and finally Warren agreed to see him. They got along very well on that first date in August 1947, and they had more dates in the weeks and months ahead, but they were too busy with their respective careers (Warren was a fashion coordinator at a major department store) to get serious.

A Hot Economy and a Cold War

With the war over, America was able to offer assistance to the European nations who were trying to rebuild. President Harry S. Truman led the way in this area with the **Marshall Plan**, named for Truman's secretary of state, George Marshall, and designed largely under Marshall's guidance. The Marshall Plan not only helped European nations get back on their feet, but also created new opportunities for American businesses to sell their products and services to them, which in turn created scores of new jobs. Similarly, during this time new products designed to create an easier and more comfortable domestic lifestyle had been developed, including cars and household appliances. Millions of Americans wanted to take advantage of these innovations. Demand skyrocketed.

The only dark cloud that lingered for America was a growing tension with the government of the Soviet Union—a tension that eventually became known as the **cold war**. No sooner had World War II ended than the leaders of both nations began to disagree over who would control what in the "new" Europe following the war. Each side was deeply suspicious of the other—the Soviet Union's leader Joseph Stalin feared that America

Joseph Stalin was the general secretary of the Communist Party of the Soviet Union.

Joseph Stalin—Another Hitler?

Soviet leader Joseph Stalin had some eerie similarities to Adolf Hitler, most notably in his thirst for control of his people and his capacity for cruelty. Toward the end of the 1930s, he undertook a campaign called the Great Purge to eliminate anyone who disagreed with his policies or otherwise threatened his power. Experts disagree on a general number, but it is believed anywhere from half a million to two million people were murdered in the Great Purge, including the poor, the handicapped, and anyone who Stalin believed was of inferior ethnicity.

would try to integrate democracy and capitalism into all of Europe in an attempt to take over the region and, essentially, turn it into an extension of itself. President Harry Truman, conversely, wanted to make sure Stalin didn't try to overrun the war-ravaged European nations and apply his communist ideology.

Congressman and Husband

By early 1947 Ford was considering a run for public office, and becoming a member of the U.S. **Congress**. The current occupant of the position for Michigan's Fifth District was Republican Bartel J. "Barney" Jonkman. He had been there since 1940, and many of his ideas were in direct opposition to Ford's. He was a passionate isolationist in spite of the changes brought about by World War II. When President Harry Truman tried to push the Marshall Plan to help Europe rebuild itself, Jonkman sought to shoot it down. Ford felt this was a foolish approach at a time when all the nations, through advancements in everything from communication to transportation, were moving closer together.

Ford was told repeatedly that Jonkman couldn't be beat—he had too much local support, too much political power. Plus, Ford was a newcomer to the political scene. Jonkman hadn't even been challenged by another **Republican** for the last nomination (in 1946), and he went on to crush his opponent, a **Democrat**, in that election. Even Betty Warren, to whom Ford was growing ever closer, had a sense of the size of the challenge. "Jerry was expected to be wiped out," she would later write. Ford, however, was adamant that Jonkman needed to be replaced. Although Michigan was a predominantly Republican state and Ford considered himself a member of its party, he also believed that Republicans and Democrats needed to work together in order for constructive progress to be made. Ford wanted to make friends on both sides of the political fence in the ultimate interest of getting things done.

After discussing his congressional ambitions with friends and family, Ford decided to wait until the very last minute to announce his candidacy so Jonkman would have less time to react to the idea that someone wanted his job. Meanwhile, Ford's relationship with Betty Warren was developing. Ford missed her terribly while on a skiing trip in December 1947. He wrote letters and bought her gifts, and upon his return he was delighted to find that she had missed him just as much. In February 1948 he proposed. However, he said, they couldn't get married until the following autumn—he wanted to focus all his energy on the election. He would either be a U.S. congressman or he'd still be a lawyer with Butterfield, Keeney, and Amberg.

Ford finally announced his candidacy in June. Jonkman, to Ford's surprise, didn't seem the least bit worried—his confidence in winning the seat again was that high. But he miscalculated—the major issue of the time was American foreign policy, and Jonkman figured the voters would subscribe to his isolationist views. Ford, however, knew better. He spent long days on the campaign trail, hammering away at his point that isolationism was not only foolish but dangerous, and that America, now the world leader in almost every category, had to address international issues or risk certain doom. There were growing threats and new enemies to face, so they could no longer afford the luxury of wearing isolationist blinders.

Soon Ford was drawing huge and enthusiastic crowds to his speeches. He may not have been the most elegant of speakers, but the substance of his words struck the right chords with ordinary people. Jonkman, on the other hand, made the error of offending large groups who had previously supported him—such as the United Auto Workers, whose endorsement was critical in getting elected in Michigan at the time—and attacking a major Grand Rapids newspaper. As Ford later wrote, "That's when Jonkman made his fatal mistake. Instead of attacking me, he blasted the Grand Rapids *Press*. They got into a bitter fight and I was the beneficiary."

Late 1948, then, turned out to be one of the happiest times in Ford's life. In September he beat the previously unbeatable Jonkman in the Republican primary election by a more than 3-to-2 margin. On October 15, 1948, he and Betty Warren were married

in Grand Rapids' Grace Episcopal Church. Then, a few weeks later, he beat his Democratic opponent in the general election and achieved his first political dream of becoming a United States' congressman. It was time for Jerry Ford to head to Washington.

EARLY POLITICAL ADVENTURES

He and his new bride moved at the end of the year, found an apartment, and began their new life. One of Ford's first major assignments was on the **Appropriations Committee**. Since he was new to Washington politics, this was an incredibly powerful position with huge responsibilities including military spending for the Korean War.

Not long after his arrival in Washington, Ford made a decision to dedicate a good portion of his time to learning how life in the **House of Representatives** worked—that is, the realities of daily procedure and the personalities of his colleagues. Since he was an easygoing individual, he had little trouble making friends. Some looked upon him skeptically due to the fact that he was inexperienced, but most found him solid and reliable.

THE KOREAN WAR

As World War II drew to a close in mid-1945, both American and Soviet forces were entrenched in the peninsular nation of Korea. They were there to crush the Japanese occupation, which they did when Japan surrendered in that region on September 9, 1945. The looming question afterward was who would temporarily govern until Korea could form its own government? In December, America and the Soviet Union decided to try to run the country in a kind of political partnership.

Ford's colleagues on Capitol Hill found him to be a hard worker who was willing to learn the ways of the House of Representatives.

Divided by a line of latitude located thirty-eight degrees north of the equator—and thereby known as the 38th Parallel—Korea would be managed by the Soviet Union in the northern half, and America in the southern half. Unfortunately, this arrangement never reached the proposed four-year rule—each nation eventually assembled a government in their respective half that mirrored their own political views.

A Meeting of Destiny

One of the most important relationships Ford would forge during his time in the House of Representatives was with Richard M. Nixon, a second-term congressman who had beat out Jerry Voorhis, a five-time incumbent Democrat from southern California's twelfth congressional district. Ford thought of Nixon as smart, focused, and well organized, and that he had a promising future in American politics. They also shared many of the same views, strengthening their kinship. What Ford could not have predicted at the time was the powerful role Nixon would eventually play in his life.

Each side eventually wanted to return Korea to a single, unified country—but neither was willing to relinquish control of their half to the other. Thus, on June 25, 1950, North Korean forces, at the command of Kim Il-Sung, crossed the 38th Parallel with the intent of capturing southern leader Syngman Rhee and getting the remaining governmental leadership to surrender. Then the United States, along with several allied countries and with the approval of the United Nations, got involved. And for the third time in the century, America was involved in a large-scale military conflict.

FORD'S NEW RESPONSIBILITIES

In February 1952, as the war in Korea progressed, the Republican Party asked Dwight D. Eisenhower, five-star general and hero of World War II, to run for the presidency. From 1933 onward, a Democrat had occupied the White House. The Republicans felt it was time for a change, and they believed Eisenhower, who was greatly admired by the public, was the man who could deliver it in their favor. Eisenhower accepted, and he chose Richard Nixon as his vice presidential running mate. Ford was happy for his friend and vigorously supported their candidacy.

Eisenhower won the election in 1952 and took office in January 1953. Ford, as reward for his loyalty to the Eisenhower/Nixon campaign, was given expanded responsibilities on the Appropriations Committee. He had greater decision-making power concerning army spending, plus funding for the Central Intelligence Agency (CIA). Ford's role at home was also expanding, becoming a father for the first time with the birth of his son, Michael, in 1950, followed by a second son,

Vice presidential candidate Richard Nixon (right) and presidential nominee Dwight D. Eisenhower celebrate at a Republican rally in September 1952.

Jack, in 1952. He and Betty would have a third son, Steven, in 1956, then a fourth and final child, Susan, in 1957. Having such a large family delighted Betty Ford, who said after Steven's birth, "I was anxious to have a third child because Jerry was so devoted to Mike and Jack."

The Fords pose for a family portrait in May 1958.

By 1958 the Republican Party had begun to lose popularity with the American people. A mild economic downturn had gripped the nation, driving them to call for a change in leadership. Furthermore, the Republicans had taken on the unpleasant image of a party of tired old men, whereas the Democrats were selling themselves as youthful and energetic. With Eisenhower's second and final term coming to an end, the Republicans chose Richard

Nixon to run in the presidential election. He would be up against the Democrats' John Fitzgerald Kennedy, senator from Massachusetts. Kennedy was a handsome young man from a wealthy Catholic family. Like Ford (and Nixon), he had also been in the House of Representatives (and eventually became a senator as well). Although they were members of opposite political parties, Kennedy and Ford got along well and shared similar views on several issues. As the 1960 election drew near, Nixon appeared to have a slim lead over Kennedy. However, Kennedy would go on to win the election that November.

For the next three years, Ford continued his many duties as congressman and father. On November 22, 1963, President Kennedy was assassinated while riding in his limousine through Dealey Plaza in Dallas, Texas. Following the Constitutional rules of succession, the presidency was taken over by Kennedy's vice president, Lyndon B. Johnson.

While the nation tried to recover from the shock, Ford was asked by Johnson to take part in an official investigation into the assassination. The group that ran it was headed by the Chief Justice of the United States Supreme Court, Earl Warren, and thus became known as the **Warren Commission**. Ford and the others worked tirelessly on the investigation, poring over thousands of documents, interviewing more than five hundred witnesses, and examining about 3,100 pieces of evidence. Their final report of nearly nine hundred pages concluded that President Kennedy was assassinated by a single gunman named Lee Harvey Oswald. In the years ahead, many would challenge the findings of the Warren Commission, claiming that Kennedy was in fact the victim of a conspiracy. But Ford and his colleagues never waivered from their

President Johnson asked Ford (far left) to participate in an investigation of the Kennedy assassination. The group that led the investigation was called the Warren Commission.

conclusions. Ford later said of these accusations, "When the report came out, critics charged that it was a whitewash, that we had covered up government complicity in the President's death. They make the same charges today. Nonsense!"

THE NEW MINORITY LEADER

The Democrats did well in the 1964 elections, gaining more seats in both the **Senate** and the House of Representatives while Lyndon Johnson won the presidency. Meanwhile, Ford was asked if he'd be interested in a new position—**House Minority Leader**. He would decide what issues would be discussed in the House, what strategies to use to reach his party's objectives, and so on. He would also work closely with the **House Majority Leader** to forge compromises between the two sides.

Ford was comfortable with his current responsibilities, so he was hesitant to accept the offer. On the other hand, there was one aspect to the job he found hard to resist—it moved him much closer to his ultimate goal of becoming the **Speaker of the House**. It is a position of tremendous power and influence. So Ford accepted the offer and was eventually chosen by his fellow House Republicans over the existing Minority Leader, Charlie Halleck, by a vote of 73–67.

THE VIETNAM WAR

The Korean War ended in July 1953 with no definitive victor, only a cease-fire agreement. Once the agreement was signed, two distinct nations were established—North and South Korea, separated by a demilitarized zone that closely, but not strictly, follows the 38th Parallel.

The United States was now a war-weary nation, but that didn't stop its leadership from getting involved in yet another conflict. The Asian nation of Vietnam was governed by the European nation of France throughout the early part of the twentieth century. That changed in 1940 when Vietnam was invaded by Japanese troops during World War II. When Japan surrendered at the end of World War II (in 1945), the United States figured Vietnam would return to its previous colonial relationship with France.

But Vietnamese leader Ho Chi Minh, who was a communist, had different intentions. He saw an opportunity to turn Vietnam into an independent country. The United States became alarmed and didn't want Vietnam to fall under Minh's control. If that happened, they feared, then communism might spread to other Asian nations as well. So the United States decided to support the Vietnamese people who opposed Minh. They also helped the French fight Minh's forces throughout the mid-1940s and into the 1950s. Minh's armies, however, proved tougher than expected, and France never did regain control. Instead, a temporary agreement was reached in 1954 that split Vietnam into two parts—North Vietnam, governed by Minh and his communist followers, and South Vietnam, eventually governed by an emperor named Ngo Dinh Diem.

Diem eventually became very unpopular with most of the Vietnamese people. Using his military forces, he stole land from farmers, executed people who opposed him, and gave preferential treatment to wealthy people over the poor. Most of the South Vietnamese citizens wanted Diem out of office, and he began to lose control. Then he was assassinated in November of 1963, plunging South Vietnam into even greater instability.

In early 1964 President Johnson considered getting America more involved in the fighting. First, however, he needed a reason that the American people would support. He found one on August 2, when an American warship was fired upon by a smaller North Vietnamese vessel in the Gulf of Tonkin. Johnson sent more American warships into the region in response. Then a second attack supposedly occurred on August 4—however, it is now believed this never happened. Nevertheless, Johnson used it as justification for sending American forces into the heart of the Vietnamese conflict.

The war progressed for the next four years, and never with a clear picture of who was winning or losing. Eventually the American people became frustrated and angry. They demanded to know why the war was dragging on so long, when it would end, and whether or not the American government had been fully truthful about the reasons for being there in the first place.

Protesters demonstrate at an anti-Vietnam War rally in Washington, D.C., in 1969.

Johnson eventually made several attempts to calm the public. In speeches, he implied that an end was in sight, and that he was confident of a positive outcome. Then, in January of 1968, came an attack known as the Tet Offensive—a massive and unexpected assault on American and South Vietnamese troops. The cost in human, military, and economic terms was enormous, and it motivated more people in America to become involved in the antiwar movement than ever before.

PRESIDENT NIXON

By 1968 the Democratic Party was in shambles. The public was enraged by what they now perceived as outright deceit on the part of President Johnson concerning the Vietnam War. Furthermore, it appeared as though the Democrats would nominate Johnson's vice president, Hubert Humphrey, to run for president in the 1968 election—and Humphrey was determined to stay the course in Vietnam. During the Democratic National Convention in Chicago, there was rioting in the streets as political protesters clashed with police. Much of this was captured on television, horrifying the nation.

Republican leaders met to discuss their nominee for the presidency, and again they chose Richard Nixon. Gerald Ford was asked if he'd be interested in the vice presidency, but he declined the offer—since the Democrats were in such a state of disarray, he felt as though Republicans would gain enough seats in the House of Representatives to earn back the majority. If that happened, he was confident his Republican friends in the House would elect him Speaker. In the end, Nixon chose the governor of Maryland, Spiro Agnew, as his running mate. Nixon ended up

President Nixon briefs House Minority Leader Gerald Ford.

beating Humphrey for the presidency, but the Republicans only gained five seats in the House of Representatives—far short of the thirty-one needed to take back the majority. Thus, Ford had to continue his duties as Minority Leader.

It wasn't long after Nixon took office that Ford began experiencing some difficulties with the new president's people. Whereas past presidents and their aides would try to work with the House and the Senate to find common ground and reach compromises in order to get things done, the Nixon officials seemed to adopt an "if you're not with us, you're against us" attitude, viewing anyone who didn't agree with them as an enemy. There were times when Ford couldn't get them to compromise on certain points, and other times when he couldn't even get them to talk to him or other members of the House. This not only frustrated Ford, it angered and alienated his colleagues. He thought it was a foolish way to do business, and he sensed trouble ahead.

MAKING HISTORY ... TWICE

On June 17, 1972, there was a break-in at Washington, D.C.'s **Watergate** complex. A security guard contacted local police, who caught five men attempting to steal sensitive documents and bug telephones in the offices of the Democratic National Committee. It was soon discovered that the men were associated with President Nixon's Committee to Re-elect the President (also known as CRP, or, more derisively, CREEP).

Ford was both stunned and upset when he heard about this, and he wanted to know whether or not anyone in Nixon's White House had known about the crime. If so, Ford said, the president should immediately fire those people. If he didn't, his reputation would be in jeopardy. President Nixon assured the American people, as well as his family and colleagues, that he had absolutely nothing to do with it.

Ford believed the president was telling the truth and continued to support him publicly. They were longtime friends, and Ford had always admired Nixon's political skills. Nixon had scored some recent political victories, which Ford wholeheartedly supported. His National Security Adviser, Henry Kissinger, had secret talks with a North Vietnamese diplomat named Le Duc Tho to formally end the Vietnam War. Also, to alleviate some of the tension in the cold war between the United States and the Soviet Union, Nixon took part in extensive negotiations to reduce each nation's stockpile of nuclear weapons. This American-Soviet cooperation would eventually become known as **détente**. And he visited China in 1972 to repair the diplomatic relationship that had been damaged since China became communist in 1949. It was a brilliant move, as it strengthened America's presence in Asia by turning China into an ally, which in turn put more pressure on Russia to cooperate with America on other issues.

THE VICE PRESIDENCY

As friendly as Ford was with President Nixon, he was not at all close to Nixon's vice president, Spiro Agnew—and Agnew was about to make Nixon's headaches worse. In August of 1973, the *Wall Street Journal* ran a story saying that Agnew had taken bribes and kickbacks while he was governor of Maryland, and possibly even as vice president.

In October, Ford was asked to visit President Nixon at the White House. Nixon gave him the ugly details of Agnew's crimes, including a few that actually occurred *in* the White House. Ford was, again, speechless. "I listened in utter astonishment as Nixon described the cash payouts that Agnew had allegedly received."

With legal action looming and the pressures of Watergate already putting a strain on Nixon's credibility, Agnew knew there was only one thing to do—on October 10, 1973, he resigned the vice presidency. Nixon was then eager to cleanse his administration's public image, and to do that he needed a new vice president—someone whose reputation was beyond question. "The nicest thing about Jerry Ford," said friend Robert Griffin, a senator from Michigan, "is that he just doesn't have enemies."

This was perfect for Nixon's needs. On the night after Agnew's resignation, a White House aide picked up the telephone and, on President Nixon's instructions, called Jerry Ford.

Up to this point, Ford had been thinking about retirement. When Nixon's popularity was running high at the end of 1972, Ford figured the Republicans would also win the majority of seats in the House of Representatives, and he would finally achieve his cherished dream of becoming Speaker—but it didn't happen. So he and his wife forged a plan—he would try to get reelected to his congressional seat one last time, then announce his retirement the following year (1975). He'd be in his early sixties and still healthy, and he could find plenty of things to keep himself busy.

Now that he was facing the possibility of being the new vice president, Ford had to rethink everything. He was deeply flattered by the offer, but he was also cautious. He would later write, "Traditionally, the Vice President didn't have much to do. His job was chiefly ceremonial and his impact on legislation was minimal. I wasn't sure that I'd be happy working at a slower pace." Ford was also concerned about changes in his family life, "I had to consider how it would affect the children. They'd be more exposed to the press; their lives would be more regulated in almost every respect."

On the other hand, Ford felt the vice presidency would be the perfect ending to his long and productive political career. He believed he could use the position to help revive Nixon's presidency and heal some old wounds in the House and Senate left behind by former members of Nixon's administration. Also, the vice president acted as overseer of the Senate, plus he had to be

NOT THE FIRST CHOICE

Ford was to learn later that he hadn't been Nixon's first choice to replace Spiro Agnew as vice president. The three others he considered before Ford were former Texas governor John Connally, former California governor Ronald Reagan, and then-current New York governor Nelson Rockefeller. Connally was Nixon's top preference, but he felt he would have some trouble getting Congress to confirm him.

ready to assume the role of president in the event the actual president could not do so. Ford felt he could handle both of these responsibilities. He accepted the offer, and his nomination was announced to Congress two days after Agnew's resignation—on October 12. Congress would, by law, have to approve the nomination first, but no problems were expected.

New problems were, however, developing with the Watergate scandal. During the investigation, it was revealed that there were recording devices set up all through the White House, and therefore most conversations—including those of President Nixon—were taped. The judge in charge of the case asked for eight tapes in particular. Nixon, however, refused to hand them over. When the prosecutor in the case insisted, Nixon ordered the attorney general of the United States to fire him. The reaction of the American people when they heard about this was so overwhelmingly hostile that Nixon, fearful of further tarnishing his image, ended up handing over the tapes anyway.

While all of this was happening, Gerald Ford was undergoing a laborious confirmation process for the vice presidency. The FBI, for example, utilized roughly 350 agents and interviewed over 1,000 people in an attempt to get a detailed picture of his past. His friends were questioned, his financial records were examined, and his political dealings were scrutinized. Then he had to sit before Congress and answer dozens of questions, all designed to find out if he was suitable for the position of vice president. On December 6, the process came to an end—the Senate had already confirmed him by a vote of 92–3 on November 27, and now the House finished the confirmation with a vote of 387–35. Ford took the oath of office the same evening and began what he

Gerald Ford is sworn in as vice president by Chief Justice Warren Burger on December 6, 1973.

believed would be the final job of his political career. In his speech immediately after being sworn in as vice president, Ford graciously acknowledged that he was not a "flashy" politician. "I am a Ford, not a Lincoln," he said. "My addresses will never be as eloquent as Mr. [Abraham] Lincoln's."

He began his vice presidential career by absorbing as much information about the state of the government as he could. He held meetings on the military, the budget, and the future of the Republican Party. Ford was also concerned about the health of the nation's economy. Unemployment was rising, as was the price of everything from food to fuel to clothing—an economic condition known as **inflation**. The spending explosion of the 1940s and 1950s had slowed, and now supply exceeded demand in many areas. Also, almost twice as many people were out of work, which meant American productivity was also sagging.

Ever supportive of the president and the Republican Party, Ford spent a great deal of time as vice president traveling around the country giving speeches. On the surface, the intention was to talk about the president's ideas for solving the nation's biggest problems, and he spoke with crowds of any size. He visited forty states and made hundreds of speeches. Unfortunately, he often found himself wasting valuable time answering questions about Watergate instead of more important matters.

Ford also decided to use the vice presidency to improve the cold image of the White House due to Nixon's habit of refusing almost all visitors and rarely appearing in public. Everyone from senators and representatives to ambassadors from around the world were welcome to stop into Ford's office. He also made a point of keeping in touch with his many friends in Congress, often having breakfast or lunch with them in order to catch up on the latest developments.

Ironically, his association with Nixon became somewhat frosty. When he was publicly asked about more tapes being requested as part of the Watergate investigation, Ford said he

Vice President Ford and his wife Betty greet ambassadors at a diplomatic reception the Fords hosted.

felt the president should fully cooperate so he could get the matter settled, clear his name, and move on to more important things. Nixon became angry with Ford for this, saying that he felt presidential conversations should always remain confidential. This put Ford in a very difficult position. He later said, "If I was critical of Nixon, people would have said, 'He's trying to get his job.' If I were not critical, people were saying I was part of the conspiracy."

Ford was also having trouble working with Nixon's staff on simple matters such as hiring people to work for him, getting enough office space, and even finding desks and chairs. Ford became equally frustrated when he held meetings with leaders of various ethnic groups—something he felt Nixon had not done often enough—then passed along his recommendations to Nixon's top people, only to have them ignored.

The vice presidency, as it turned out, wasn't running as smoothly for Ford as he'd hoped.

THE 1973 OIL CRISIS

In October of 1973 the organization of Arab nations that provided millions of barrels of oil to countries around the world announced that they would no longer ship their product to anyone who was supporting Israel during that year's Arab-Israeli War. One of the countries deeply affected by this decision was the United States. As a result, gas prices skyrocketed, oil from other sources could only be acquired in limited quantities, and the American economy suffered on all fronts. Auto manufacturers began making cars with smaller, more fuel-efficient engines, and people had to wait in long lines to fill up their tanks. It began a new chapter in the uneasy business relationship between the Arab world and the West that sustains to this day.

A Second Moment in History

In February Ford met with Nixon to discuss several important national matters. But the Watergate scandal had recently reared its ugly head again—it was determined that 18.5 minutes of one of the tapes Nixon eventually gave to investigators had been erased, probably intentionally. Distracted by this, Nixon babbled about insignificant things. This frustrated Ford, who found it alarming behavior for a leader whose honesty was being questioned and whose country was struggling with serious problems.

Nixon and Ford discuss the transfer of the presidency.

But Nixon assured Ford, once again, that he had nothing to do with the Watergate break-in, and that evidence would soon come to light to clear his name. Ford wanted to believe this, but now he was growing unsure.

In early June the president was officially named as a co-conspirator in the Watergate burglary. A month later, Ford tried again to talk with him on important national matters, and again he found Nixon unable to focus. Nixon knew one of the tapes contained a conversation that confirmed not only that he had full knowledge of the Watergate break-in, but that he directed an effort to hinder the FBI's investigation of it. The final blow came on July 30, when Congress voted to impeach Nixon, removing him from power. Rather than suffer that humiliation, Nixon became the first and only U.S. president to resign from office, which he did on August 9, 1974. As a result, Ford, the reliable young man from the humble Michigan town, was now the leader of the free world.

PICKING UP THE PIECES

*T*he moral conflict Ford had with this relatively quick two-step ascension to power was that he now held the highest office in America, yet he hadn't been selected by the American citizens. It was the first and only time an individual reached the presidency without ever having spent a minute campaigning for the job. Ford feared that he would not have the confidence of the American people. In his inaugural address to the nation, he said, "I am acutely aware that you have not elected me as your president by your ballots, and so I ask you to confirm me as your president in your prayers." His other major concern involved the ghost of Nixon. Even though the man was no longer in the White House, would Congress and the rest of the American citizens feel a certain bias toward Ford regardless of how efficiently and effectively he ran his own presidency? "The Nixon presidency dragged the public's trust in government down to a new low," wrote Ford biographer Yanek Mieczkowski.

MAKING AMENDS

Not wanting the Nixon specter to loom over his administration and possibly paralyze his efforts, Ford made it clear his presidency would not simply be an extension of Nixon's, but one that was markedly new and improved.

He began with the elimination of all Nixon people in the White House who had contributed to ugly moods and unprofes-

President Ford takes a call in the Oval Office. The bookshelves are still empty since Nixon left only two days earlier.

sional tactics. Ford did, however, keep all members of Nixon's Cabinet not only because he wanted to maintain continuity and utilize their experience, but also because they were genuinely good people who'd had nothing to do with the Watergate scandal.

Ford refused to punish anyone who hadn't done anything wrong; simply being associated with Nixon wasn't a good enough reason to remove them. This kind of fairness endeared him to the people on his staff.

He also went out of his way to restore relations with members of Congress, which had been badly damaged by Nixon. Having spent so many years in the House of Representatives, Ford knew these people well. He had no intention of throwing away the decades of hard work he'd spent forging friendships and building alliances. Even when he disagreed with someone on an important issue, he didn't let things get personal—he often said he had many adversaries in Congress, but no enemies. Ford promised an open-door policy where he would meet with key congressional members several times a week. He would later say, "Nixon, by nature, was a recluse who preferred to deal with problems through paperwork rather than through people. I don't do business that way." And he would do more than just talk—he'd *listen*. Ford also insisted that his legislative liaisons (people who acted as the lines of communication between himself and Congress) behave in a respectable manner, and he expressed full confidence in their abilities. If a member of Congress spoke with one of Ford's liaisons, they could be certain their messages would be faithfully delivered to the president.

The press, the public, and the U.S. Congress responded favorably to all these changes during the first few weeks of Ford's administration, and it seemed he was going to successfully exorcise the dark spirit of Nixon.

But then it came back.

President Ford talks with economists and senators at a White House conference.

BEGGING YOUR PARDON

From the moment he took office, Ford was bombarded with questions about Nixon's future—would he be dragged into court, would the investigation continue, was there a possibility of imprisonment, and so on. Ford was more interested in discussing the key challenges facing his administration—rising prices and

A More Relaxed White House

Ford knew changes had to be made on a social level in the White House if the image of the presidency was to be cleansed—it could no longer appear cold and stiff. Nixon, for example, rarely held social events. Ford, on the other hand, threw many parties and invited hundreds of guests. He wanted these occasions to be enjoyable and fun—something Nixon rarely did and severely disliked. Ford and his wife, Betty, would often stay up late with friends and family, chatting and dancing.

unemployment, the fuel crisis, America's relationship with China and the Soviet Union, the final steps to the Vietnam issue—but the media wanted to keep the Nixon/Watergate story alive.

Finally, on September 8—less than a month after taking over as president—Ford attempted to put the matter to rest. On television that morning, he announced to the nation that he would grant Nixon a full and unconditional **pardon**. According to the U.S. Constitution's Article II, Section 2, the president has the power to "grant reprieves and pardons for offenses against the United States." In simple terms, this means the president can relieve a person of any legal penalties stemming from criminal activity. Pardons can also be given in varying degrees, for example, where a sentence or a fine is reduced rather than altogether eliminated. In this instance, Ford immunized Nixon from any punishment arising from his involvement in the Watergate burglary.

While Nixon was undoubtedly relieved, the reaction on all other fronts was one of shock and outrage. The press figuratively broiled Ford alive, suggesting his moral appearance was nothing but a front for the underhanded Nixon. Editorials claimed his credibility and honorability were permanently marred, and that he had committed a flagrant abuse of executive power. First Lady Betty Ford later wrote, "The very next day after the pardon, he went to Pittsburgh . . . and he was booed by critics who thought he'd made a deal." The public had hoped the process of justice would play out as required, for Nixon had broken the law and should be tried like anyone else— he had betrayed the voters, so he should receive a suitable punishment. With the pardon, Ford saved him from this.

President Ford announces his pardon of Richard Nixon.

Protesters demonstrate in opposition to Nixon's pardon.

Inevitably, speculation arose about the possibility of a deal having been made between the two men, that is, had Nixon promised Ford the presidency under the condition that Ford would grant the pardon? There apparently was a meeting between Ford and Nixon's chief of staff, Alexander Haig, where Haig suggested the pardon, but Ford rejected the idea at the time.

Many historians find this believable based on Ford's own political and personal history.

Ford went before the press and said that he had decided to focus his energies on the problems and issues facing the vast majority of Americans rather than waste it on the controversy surrounding one man. For better or worse, he wanted to put the matter in the past and get on with the business of governing the country. He would later write, "I felt very certain that I had made the right decision, and I was confident that I could now proceed without being harassed by Nixon or his problems anymore." Ford also made the courageous choice to sit before Congress in October of 1974 and give testimony to his reasons for the pardon. He insisted, in full view of millions of Americans, that no deal had been made between him and the former president. It was a chance for the public to judge his character, even if they hadn't had the chance to vote for him.

In the end, in spite of his admirable openness and sincere pragmatism, his credibility took a huge hit. Polls suggested that nearly 60 percent of the public disagreed with the pardon, and Ford's approval rating—which is determined by polls taken among the American people—sank more than 20 percentage points. The press never showed him the same level of trust, and many of the congressional politicians he had worked so hard to befriend once again became bitter and resentful.

Only a few months into Ford's presidency the **midterm elections** appeared on the horizon, and very little had gone right thus far. When election day finally arrived—November 5, 1974— the Republican Party, unsurprisingly, suffered huge losses. In the Senate, Democrats, already the majority, picked up three more

THE RADIOACTIVE PRESIDENT

Traditionally, a sitting president will join prospective senators and representatives on their campaign trails in order to lend his support. Since the pardoning of Nixon, however, Ford was considered "radioactive," which meant an appearance from him might actually harm a congressional candidate rather than help. In places where Ford did campaign, he was often greeted with boos and jeers.

seats, giving them a 61–39 advantage. But it was the House results that really hurt Ford—Democrats picked up 49 new seats, giving them a total of 291 versus the Republicans' 144. The most significant aspect of this radical shift in power was that the Democrats now controlled more than two-thirds of the House—the amount required to override a presidential veto. This was a major blow to Ford's executive abilities.

Ford still had a few friends in the House, but not enough. Many had either retired or lost their seat to someone Ford didn't know. Furthermore, the average age of the House members had dropped to its lowest number in years—and these freshman politicians only associated Ford with the Watergate debacle. They were a new generation with a new attitude, and many walked through the House doors for the first time with a "beat Ford at any cost" chip on their shoulders. Evidence of this was seen during Ford's State of the Union address in 1975, when several "youngsters" had the audacity to walk out of the House chamber before the president was finished speaking.

Publicly, Ford was still upbeat and promised to work with this new Democratic majority.

A STILL-STRUGGLING ECONOMY

One black cloud that loomed over Ford's administration was the struggling American economy. With economic growth slowing to a crawl, ordinary citizens were beginning to feel real financial pain. There were shortages of food, fuel, and other essential commodities, plus instability in many leading industries, including auto manufacturing, housing, and farming. Perhaps most menacing, the United States was hit by a previously unseen one-two punch of economic conditions—both inflation and unemployment were rising. Rising prices usually meant lower unemployment, because higher prices also created new jobs. During the early and mid-1970s, however, both prices *and* joblessness increased, inspiring a new term—**stagflation**. It also pushed the misery index (an economic indicator created by the combined sum of inflation and unemployment) to its highest levels ever. And while Ford told the public he was dedicated to finding a cure for inflation, an even uglier situation was threatening to emerge—**recession**.

Ford knew of the recession threat and wanted to avoid it at all costs. His first major effort to improve the economy, announced in early October of 1974, was known as the WIN campaign. WIN stood for Whip Inflation Now, and the idea behind it was a **grassroots** movement to reduce the amount of excessive consumption among average Americans. And not just luxury items, but necessities such as food and fuel. At one point Ford told the public, "If we all drive at least five percent fewer miles, we can save, almost unbelievably, 250,000 barrels of foreign oil per day." Ford also urged citizens to curtail the waste of food, electricity, and water. As well intentioned as the plan may have been, it simply didn't work. Asking people in a staggered economy to make further sacrifices was a long shot, and the fact that the nation was still fuming over the Nixon pardon didn't exactly inspire people to give Ford's idea much of a chance.

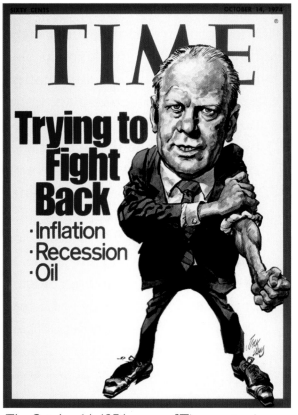

The October 14, 1974, cover of Time *magazine illustrates Ford ready to take on inflation, recession, and the shortage of oil.*

The economy continued to worsen, and by the end of 1974 the facts spoke for themselves—companies were laying off workers by the thousands, production levels were dropping off, and people began expressing their anger. By April the unemployment rate was nearing 9 percent—meaning almost one out of every ten Americans did not have a job. Experts were claiming the worst economic climate since the Great Depression. Ford, knowing extreme measures were required, held meetings with dozens of economic experts, business leaders, and other top politicians, gathering information and opinions in a desperate search for an effective plan. In the end, he felt he had no choice but to cut federal taxes. This gave ordinary people some relief because it meant they could keep more money for themselves rather than give it to the government. But it also meant there was less money for government programs, so Ford had to cut many of those as well.

By October 1975 the economy had not improved nearly as much as Ford had hoped, so he asked Congress for more cuts in taxes and federal spending. Since Congress was still under control of the Democratic Party (who traditionally champion federal programs more often than Republicans), Ford's request met with stiff resistance. Congress had no trouble with the idea of further tax cuts, but they were opposed to a further reduction in programs. Many were designed to help the poor and underprivileged, and President Ford was sensitive to this. But part of being president required making difficult decisions—including those where no perfect solution was available. In the end, the Democratic Congress made several adjustments to Ford's request for program reduction, and Ford eventually approved the plan.

THE END GAME IN VIETNAM

Once military action between America and North Vietnam was halted in 1973, American military troops withdrew from the region and returned home. And North Vietnamese leaders realized they wouldn't come back under any circumstances—the war had caused such outrage in America, the American citizens simply would not allow it to flare up again. As if to provide proof of this, American voters flooded Washington with Democrats in the 1974 midterm elections—Democrats who remembered the beating their own party took in 1968 over the same issue. The Vietnam War had also been the most costly in history—over $150 billion—and would cost billions more to revive. In the middle of an economic blight, no sensible politician would support such a notion.

With all of this in mind, the North Vietnamese decided to ignore the peace agreement and launch a new wave of attacks in early January 1975. Ford begged Congress for funding to support South Vietnam, but to no avail—they declined all such requests, and Ford's hands were tied.

By March of 1975 North Vietnamese forces had made tremendous progress, overwhelming their weakened opponent and occupying huge territories. Ford held meetings with his military advisors to see what could be done, but by this time it was too late—he was told it was only a matter of time before North Vietnam penetrated the South's capital city of Saigon. Once that happened, it would be over. On April 21 Nguyen Van Thieu resigned as president and fled to Europe. Two days later, Ford made a speech essentially reversing the position he'd held on Vietnam all along. "Today, America can regain the sense of pride that existed before Vietnam. But it cannot be achieved by refighting a war that is finished as far as America is concerned." He was applauded not only by the immediate audience, but by the nation as a whole. At last, the Vietnam conflict was officially over—the president of the United States just said so.

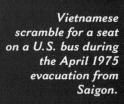

Vietnamese scramble for a seat on a U.S. bus during the April 1975 evacuation from Saigon.

The final step in Ford's mind was to evacuate the remaining American citizens and South Vietnamese people who had loyally served America. At first this required military planes to fly in and out of the airport at Saigon. When North Vietnamese forces began firing upon them, however, the plan switched to helicopters carrying people off the roof of the American Embassy, plus rescuing the thousands of South Vietnamese who were trying to escape by sea in boats that were far too small to have any chance of reaching America. In the end, about 40,000 people left via the Saigon airport, another 7,500 from the embassy rooftop, and about 32,000 more were picked up by naval ships in the open ocean.

BRILLIANCE IN HELSINKI

At the end of July 1975 Ford went to Helsinki, Finland, to attend the Conference for Security and Cooperation in Europe (CSCE). Representatives from over thirty nations (mostly from Europe and Asia) attended, and the purpose was to settle bitter differences on three separate issues—border disputes, free trade, and human rights. The Soviet Union was a key player in all three. They wanted to open channels of free trade with other nations, plus exchange ideas on scientific and cultural fronts. Concerning human rights, however, they had put themselves in a poor position because they had oppressed many of their own citizens for everything from speaking out against their communist government to practicing religions their government had abolished.

Ford's decision to attend the CSCE angered many in the United States. Some criticized him for even being willing to sit down with Soviet leadership. Ford was trying to diffuse the tension of the cold war, but some didn't want it diffused. The Soviet

Union was America's sworn enemy, they said, and to cut a deal with Soviet leaders was akin to treason. One former Soviet citizen, a Nobel Prize-winning author who had immigrated to the United States after writing about harsh treatment of dissidents by the Soviet government, asked to meet with Ford before the trip. Ford refused, and he was publicly criticized.

But Ford saw a tremendous opportunity that others did not. Choosing to remain flexible on the border and free-trade issues, he got the Soviet leadership to agree not only to loosening its grip on its people, but also to allow watchdog groups into the country to make sure these promises were kept. This was essentially the beginning of the end of communism in the Soviet

President Ford signs documents to bring a close to the European Security Conference Summit in Helsinki, Finland.

Union—once Soviet citizens enjoyed true freedom, they would use it like a pickax to gradually chip away their government's control. Ford knew personal freedom was the heart of a democratic society, and he gave it to the Soviet people through his

ASSASSINATION ATTEMPTS

There were two assassination attempts on Gerald Ford's life during his presidency. Strangely, they took place less than three weeks apart.

The first occurred in Sacramento, California's, Capitol Park on September 5, 1975. Lynette Fromme, a member of a bizarre counterculture cult that would eventually be held responsible for many grisly murders, pointed a semi-automatic pistol at Ford as he walked just two feet away. An astute Secret Service agent managed to keep the gun from firing while other agents swarmed Fromme, pulling her to the ground and handcuffing her. Fromme was tried and convicted of an assassination attempt on a U.S. president and sentenced to life in prison.

The second occurred seventeen days later, on September 22. A forty-five-year-old former nursing student and accountant, Sara Jane Moore, while standing across the street from Ford as he emerged from the St. Francis Hotel in downtown San Francisco, California, fired one pistol shot from a distance of about forty feet. Fortunately, a bystander spotted the gun and grabbed for it just before Moore pulled the trigger. The deflected shot ricocheted off both a wall and a curb before a bystander, causing a minor injury. Ironically, it was later revealed that Moore was also a secret informant for the FBI. Like Fromme, she received a life sentence.

In 1976 Ford decided to run for a second term as president of the United States.

influence at the Helsinki meeting. In years to come, historians would applaud this as a brilliant move.

Looking Toward a Second Term

By 1976 Ford began considering his campaign for another term as president. Looking back on the first one, he had some doubts. His pardoning of Richard Nixon had cost him dearly in terms of political clout. In spite of all the time that had passed, reporters still wrote about it, and people in the street still talked about it. His previously shining reputation as a man of honesty and principle had been tarnished with that one act, even if he still believed it was the proper thing to do. He wondered how much it would affect his chances of winning the election in November. Also, the economy was finally beginning to show signs of improvement—but the nation had still gone through the most painful economic period since the Great Depression. And many conservative members of Ford's party seemed to have given up their support of him due to his moderate policies—policies Ford felt would help ordinary Americans and address social issues in a sensible, open-minded manner. With all these potential barriers in mind, did he really have a chance of being elected president in 1976? He decided to find out.

LATER YEARS

Six

In order for Ford to recapture the White House in the 1976 elections, he would have to fend off not just an eventual challenger from the Democratic Party, but a right-wing challenger from his own party. In order to do that, he figured, he would have to change his moderate, middle-of-the-road image to something more in line with the Republicans' conservative beliefs.

PERSONNEL SHAKEUP

The first and most visible position in the administration that Ford decided to change was that of the man immediately below him—the vice president. His vice president since taking office was Nelson Rockefeller, former governor of New York, philanthropist, and multimillionaire businessman from one of the wealthiest American families in history. He was also one of the leading voices from the liberal side of the Republican Party, which is why Ford chose him after Nixon resigned—the Democrats liked him, so his nomination as vice president through Congress would be a relatively painless process. Now that the conservatives were threatening to nominate someone else for a presidential run in 1976, Ford had to consider replacing Rockefeller.

The problem was that Rockefeller had been an excellent vice president. He dutifully, and without complaint, supported Ford in all of his programs and policies. He took whatever task Ford assigned him and managed it flawlessly. He never opposed the president in public, never said anything negative or foolish to the press. He was, in most every way, a perfect vice president.

In his run for office in 1976, Ford decided to replace Vice President Rockefeller with someone who had more favor with conservatives.

But the pressure on Ford was growing, and when Rockefeller did finally make a public relations mistake in October of 1975 by altering Ford's position on an important financial crisis during a speech, Ford decided it was time for Rockefeller to go. He didn't have to pick a new person immediately, but simply tell Rockefeller he wasn't going to run with him in the 1976 election. Ever the team player, Rockefeller took the news with good grace and civility. Later on, Ford would say that he deeply regretted the decision to jettison "Rocky," as Rockefeller was fondly known. He felt he should have, instead, stood by his old friend. He would later write, "I was angry with myself for showing cowardice in not saying to the ultraconservatives, 'It's going to be Ford and Rockefeller, whatever the consequences.'"

In the end, Ford decided to go with Bob Dole as his vice presidential running mate. Dole was a popular senator from Kansas with conservative views that would keep the right wing of the Republican Party happy. He also had a clean image, that is, with no scandals, and therefore would cause the least amount of harm to Ford's reelection chances. Ford then added other new people to his administration—including chief of staff, secretary of defense,

Bob Dole waves to supporters after his acceptance speech of the vice presidential nomination.

secretary of state, and director of the CIA—all for the sake of appeasing conservatives.

Ironically, however, all these personnel changes made little difference in the end, because a tenacious and ambitious member of the Republican Party's conservative wing decided to challenge Ford for the presidential nomination anyway—former California governor Ronald Reagan.

A Narrow Victory

Reagan was born in Illinois in 1911 and started his professional career as an actor and radio broadcaster. His early political leanings were more on the Democratic side, as he was a great admirer of President Franklin Roosevelt. But then he shifted to the Republican Party after Dwight Eisenhower's presidency. He was elected twice as California's governor, but chose not to run again after 1975. Instead, he focused on becoming president—and that meant beating Ford as the Republicans' nominee in 1976. Rarely had a sitting president been challenged for his party's nomination, but Reagan thought his chances were good.

On November 20, 1975, he publicly announced his candidacy for the presidency. He then spent most of the next nine months viciously attacking Ford on every level. He emphasized Ford's mistakes, questioned his character, and criticized his personality. As a result of all this, Ford was forced to spend less time in the White House, fixing the nation's pressing problems, and more time battling Reagan. In the end, Ford still got the nomination—in August of 1976, in Kansas City, he was chosen by the Republicans over Reagan by a narrow margin. Nevertheless, Ford would never forgive Reagan for weakening

Ronald Reagan speaks at a campaign rally during the 1976 presidential primary.

him. For now, however, he had to shift his focus onto his Democratic opponent for the presidency—an easygoing farmer from Georgia who was relatively new to the political scene. His name was Jimmy Carter.

The 1976 Presidential Election

James Earl "Jimmy" Carter was born in Plains, Georgia, in 1924. He attended both Georgia Tech and Georgia Southwestern State University before joining the United States Navy. After leaving the navy in 1953, he took over his family's farming business. In 1962 he was elected to the Georgia state senate, then became governor from January of 1971 until January of 1975, at which time he decided to run for the presidency.

Few people knew who Carter was at the start of the 1976 campaign. But his easy smile, good nature, and reputation for honesty and integrity struck a chord with the average American. Ironically, this was the same image Ford had built for himself so many years earlier—but the pardoning of Nixon still haunted him, forever damaging his good-guy status. Also, Ronald Reagan's incessant harping about Ford being a Washington insider became an advantage for Carter, who never spent a moment as a professional politician in the nation's capital. The American people were ready for an outsider to come and clean things up, and to usher in a new era of federal government. In spite of Carter's inexperience in federal matters (and a complete lack of experience in foreign affairs), American citizens were desperate for a change. Carter knew this and played upon it. He and Ford went head to head during three nationally televised debates. In the first, Ford edged out Carter largely because he was more experienced and managed to present himself presidentially. Carter, however, learned from the loss and came back with a vengeance in the second. Ford also made some crucial errors when speaking about foreign affairs,

President Ford and his challenger, Georgia Governor Jimmy Carter, during their second presidential debate on October 6, 1976.

creating the appearance that he was out of touch with the voters and their problems.

According to the polls, Carter and Ford were neck and neck right up to Election Day—November 2, 1976. In fact, on the day before, most polls suggested Ford still held a slim lead. But when all the votes were counted, Carter had defeated him with 297 electoral votes versus the president's 240. Although the campaign had been long and hard fought, the two men were gracious and civil toward each other when it was over. Ford praised Carter in public, and Carter returned the gesture, saying in his inaugural address, "For myself and for our nation, I want to thank my predecessor for all he has done to heal our land."

RETIREMENT YEARS

Ford had no intention of sitting around once he left office; he was too active and curious an individual for that.

Impressed by Carter's generous words during his inauguration, Ford felt a certain kinship toward the new president, and the two became good friends. For the extent of Carter's time in office, Ford occasionally acted as consultant, advisor, and confidante, particularly on foreign affairs. Ford also wrote his memoirs, which were published in 1979, *A Time to Heal: The Autobiography of Gerald R. Ford*. He considered the idea of running for president again in the 1980 election, but ultimately decided against it. Ronald Reagan finally did get the Republican nomination that year, and there was even talk of Ford being his vice president in a kind of dual presidency. But that idea was also dismissed—Ford was content being a spectator now.

Ford continued his personal crusade to inject honesty and integrity wherever he could. He was asked to sit on the boards of many large businesses, where he often acted as a watchdog to ensure ethical behavior. Perhaps most satisfying to Ford was that the passage of time seemed to cleanse and restore his reputation. More people were beginning to understand why he made many

Former president Gerald Ford visits President Jimmy Carter in the Oval Office in May 1978. In the years ahead they would become close friends.

BETTY FORD'S REMARKABLE JOURNEY

One dark spot in the Ford's lives was Betty's struggle with alcohol and drug dependency, which began after her battle with breast cancer in the mid-1970s. Following treatment, she began taking pills for pain and recovery—but she continued to take them long after they were no longer necessary. She also drank due to depression, and because she

(continued)

had genetic tendencies toward alcoholism. Rather than let these demons defeat her, however, she and her family turned the situation into a positive—she sought professional help for herself, then decided to help others with the same problems. "I just think it's important to say how easy it is to slip into a dependency on pills and alcohol," she wrote in her memoirs. "And how hard it is to admit that dependency." The result of this courageous attitude was the Betty Ford Center. Since its opening in 1982, it has aided millions in their struggle against drug and alcohol abuse.

of the difficult decisions as president. Writers who had attacked him during his time in office were offering apologetic articles, reversing their opinions and trying to correct the record, so to speak. When President Bill Clinton was attacked by Republicans in 1998, Ford rose to his defense, scolding his own party for wasting government time on irrelevant personal issues when they should be working on matters of national interest. In May of 2001, Ford was even given the John F. Kennedy Foundation's Profiles in Courage Award—and it was presented to him by Kennedy's brother, Senator Ted Kennedy of Massachusetts. The senator had been one of Ford's most outspoken critics when he pardoned Nixon, but now he was giving Ford an award largely for the same reason—in time, people understood that the pardon was the right thing to do. But when Ford did it, he did so in the face of considerable opposition.

Final Days

Ford had enjoyed relatively good health throughout his life. By his late eighties, however, he began experiencing the unavoidable problems of old age. He suffered minor strokes in 2000, then developed heart problems. In 2006, at the age of ninety-two, he was treated for pneumonia. He was also admitted to a hospital in July for shortness of breath, followed by several surgical procedures. He didn't return home until November, at which time he was confined to his bed. With his wife and three sons at his side, he passed away on December 26, 2006.

At eighty-seven years old, Ford attended the 2000 Republican National Convention in Philadelphia. Soon after, he suffered two mild strokes.

His funeral was, like the man himself, dignified and understated. Eulogies came from friends and colleagues such as former secretary of state Henry Kissinger, former president George H. W. Bush, and former president and close friend Jimmy Carter, whose emotional delivery underscored the magnitude of the loss. But it was perhaps Ford's own words, given in a statement when he became the oldest former president in November of 2006, that defined his true self and illustrated the individual that history will eventually recognize as a genuinely great man.

> *The length of one's days matters less than the love of one's family and friends. I thank God for the gift of every sunrise and, even more, for all the years. He has blessed me with Betty and the children; with our extended family and the friends of a lifetime. That includes countless Americans who, in recent months, have remembered me in their prayers. Your kindness touches me deeply. May God bless you all and may God bless America.*

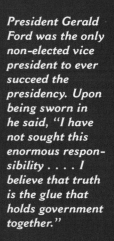

*President Gerald
Ford was the only
non-elected vice
president to ever
succeed the
presidency. Upon
being sworn in
he said, "I have
not sought this
enormous respon-
sibility I
believe that truth
is the glue that
holds government
together."*

TIMELINE

1913
Born in Omaha, Nebraska,
July 14

1930–1935
Attends the University of
Michigan, Ann Arbor

1937–1940
Attends Yale University

1942
Enlists in the U.S. Navy

1948
Wins congressional seat for
Michigan's Fifth District

1964
Elected House Minority
Leader

1900

1973
Becomes vice president

1974
Becomes president following
Richard Nixon's resignation

1976
Runs for another term as
president but loses to Georgia
governor Jimmy Carter

2001
Receives the Kennedy
Foundation's Profile in
Courage Award

2006
Passes away,
December 26

2010

NOTES

CHAPTER 1

p. 7, ". . . execute the office of the President . . ." "The United States Constitution," Microsoft Encarta, 2008.

p. 8, ". . . fellow Americans, our long national nightmare . . ." Gerald R. Ford, *A Time to Heal: The Autobiography of Gerald R. Ford*. New York: Harper & Row, 1979, p. 26.

p. 12, ". . . three great principles which Scouting encourages . . ." Boy Scouts of America National Council, "Scouts Mourn First Eagle Scout President." http://www.bsalegal .org/bsa-legal-blawg-200.asp?i=79 (accessed December 27, 2006).

CHAPTER 2

p. 18, ". . . my talents would be those of the mediator and counselor . . ." Gerald R. Ford, *A Time to Heal: The Autobiography of Gerald R. Ford*. New York: Harper & Row, 1979, pp. 53–54.

p. 19, ". . . decided to strike out on our own . . ." Ford, *A Time to Heal*, p. 57.

p. 21, ". . . needs peace#. . ." William L. Shirer, *The Rise and Fall of the Third Reich: A History of Nazi Germany*. New York: Simon and Schuster, 1960, p. 286.

p. 24, ". . . Congress declare that since the unprovoked and dastardly attack . . ." Michael Waldman, *My Fellow Americans: The Most Important Speeches of America's Presidents, from George Washington to George W. Bush*. Naperville, IL: Sourcebooks MediaFusion, 2003, p. 121.

CHAPTER 3

p. 30, ". . . experiences had given me an entirely new . . ." Gerald R. Ford, *A Time to Heal: The Autobiography of Gerald R. Ford*. New York: Harper & Row, 1979, p. 61.

p. 31, ". . . 34 years old . . ." Ford, *A Time to Heal*, p. 62.

p. 31, ". . . process of getting a divorce, and you're a lawyer . . ." Betty Ford (with Chris Chase), *The Times of My Life*. New York: Harper & Row, 1978, p. 46.

p. 34, "Jerry was expected . . ." Ford, *The Times of My Life*, p. 57.

p. 35, ". . . when Jonkman made his fatal mistake . . ." Ford, *A Time to Heal*, p. 67.

p. 41, ". . . was so anxious to have a third child . . ." J. F. ter Horst, *Gerald Ford and the Future of the Presidency*. New York: The Third Press, 1974, p. 68.

p. 44, ". . . the report came out . . ." Ford, *A Time to Heal*, p. 76.

CHAPTER 4

p. 52, ". . . in utter astonishment . . ." Gerald R. Ford, *A Time to Heal: The Autobiography of Gerald R. Ford*. New York: Harper & Row, 1979, p. 103.

p. 52, ". . . nicest thing about Jerry Ford . . ." J. F. ter Horst, *Gerald Ford and the Future of the Presidency*. New York: The Third Press, 1974, p. 215.

p. 53, ". . . the Vice President didn't have much to do . . ." Ford, *A Time to Heal*, p. 104.

p. 53, ". . . consider how it would affect the children. . . ." Ford, *A Time to Heal*, p. 104.

p. 56, ". . . a Ford, not a Lincoln . . ." Yanek Mieczkowski, *Gerald Ford and the Challenges of the 1970s*. Lexington: The University Press of Kentucky, 2005, p. 12.

p. 58, ". . . was critical of Nixon, people would have said . . ." Mieczkowski, *Gerald Ford*, p. 12.

CHAPTER 5

p. 62, ". . . acutely aware that you have not elected me as your president . . ." Douglas Brinkley, *Gerald R. Ford*. New York: Henry Holt and Company, 2007, p. 62.

p. 62, ". . . Nixon presidency dragged the public's trust . . ." Yanek Mieczkowski, *Gerald Ford and the Challenges of the 1970s*. Lexington: The University Press of Kentucky, 2005, p. 20.

p. 64, ". . . was a recluse who preferred to deal . . ." Gerald R. Ford, *A Time to Heal: The Autobiography of Gerald R. Ford*. New York: Harper & Row, 1979, p. 126.

p. 67, ". . . reprieves and pardons for offenses . . ." "The United States Constitution," Microsoft Encarta, 2008.

p. 67, ". . . very next day after the pardon . . ." Betty Ford (with Chris Chase), *The Times of My Life*. New York: Harper & Row, p. 181.

p. 70, ". . . felt very certain that I had made . . ." Ford, *A Time to Heal*, p. 178.

p. 73, ". . . drive at least five percent fewer miles . . ." Brinkley, *Gerald R. Ford*, p. 77.

p. 75, ". . . regain the sense of pride . . ." Brinkley, *Gerald R. Ford*, p. 91.

CHAPTER 6

p. 83, ". . . angry with myself for showing cowardice . . ." Gerald R. Ford, *A Time to Heal: The Autobiography of Gerald R. Ford*. New York: Harper & Row, 1979, p. 328.

p. 89, ". . . myself and for our nation . . ." Douglas Brinkley, *Gerald R. Ford*. New York: Henry Holt and Company, 2007, p. 145.

p. 92, ". . . think it's important to say how easy it is . . ." Ford, *The Times of My Life*, pp. 292–293

p. 94, ". . . length of one's days matters less . . ." Gerald Ford, Statement released from his home in Rancho Mirage, CA, November 9, 2006.

GLOSSARY

Appropriations Committee a group from the House of Representatives responsible for deciding how the money of the federal government will be spent

bar exam the test all lawyers must pass before they can receive their license to practice law

capitalism a political system through which the people work to further their individual interests, and private citizens retain ownership and control of virtually all business and industry

cold war period of increased tensions between two nations, but without military battles. Most often used to describe the relationship between the United States and the Soviet Union following World War II.

communism a political system in which the people work to further the interests of their society as a whole rather than those of each individual, and in which the government retains ownership and control of all business and industry

Congress the legislative branch of the United States government, made up of two parts—the Senate and the House of Representatives

credit a financial tool through which a person can acquire something without having to pay for it right away, with the understanding that they will pay later

Democrats one of the two major political parties in the United States. Generally considered the more liberal and progressive, and in favor of larger government.

détente a policy of increased cooperation between two nations

economy the relative financial prosperity of a nation

grassroots having to do with the common, ordinary people of a society

House Majority Leader leader of the political party that holds the majority of seats in the House of Representatives. There are currently 435 seats in the House, so the party that has 218 seats or more would be the majority.

House Minority Leader leader of the political party that holds the minority of seats in the House of Representatives. There are currently 435 seats in the House, so the party that has 217 seats or less would be the minority.

House of Representatives one of the two parts of the United States Congress; considered the lower of the two. There are 435 seats in the House, representing all 50 states.

inflation an economic situation characterized by an across-the-board rise in prices of goods and services

internationalist someone who believes that a nation should be willing to involve itself in the affairs of other nations as well as its own

isolationist someone who believes that a nation should focus on its own affairs and generally disregard those of other nations

Marshall Plan a plan designed by U. S. Secretary of State George C. Marshall in 1947 to help European nations rebuild their communities and revitalize their economies following World War II

midterm election an election held for senators, representatives, governors, and other politicians at the two-year point (that is, the middle) of a president's term of office

Nazi Party political party in Germany started in 1919. The word Nazi was short for National Socialist German Workers' Party.

pardon presidential act in which a crime against the United States is forgiven, to varying degrees depending on the wishes of the president

recession a period during which a nation's economy shows consistently sluggish growth; usually at least six consecutive months

Republican one of the two major political parties in the United States. Generally considered the more conservative and in favor of smaller government

Senate one of the two parts of the United States Congress; considered the upper of the two

Speaker of the House the spokesperson for the majority party in the House of Representatives

stagflation an economic situation in which both inflation and unemployment rise

theater in terms of warfare, a large and general geographic area in which many battles and sustained campaigns are fought

Treaty of Versailles peace agreement following World War I that required Germany to disarm its military, give up large sections of territory, pay for the damage caused by the battles, and admit to causing the war in the first place

Warren Commission seven-man group recruited by President Lyndon Johnson in 1963 to investigate the assassination of President John F. Kennedy

Watergate name of a hotel/apartment/office complex in Washington, D.C., where the infamous Watergate break-in was carried out by five political operatives under the guidance of President Richard M. Nixon

World War II second large-scale global conflict, fought mostly in European and Asian theaters from 1939–1945

FURTHER INFORMATION

BOOKS

Aronson, Billy. *Richard M. Nixon* (Presidents and Their Times). Tarrytown, NY: Marshall Cavendish Corporation, 2008.

Marcovitz, Hal. *The Vietnam War* (World History). Farmington Hills, MI: Lucent Books, 2007.

Winget, Mary Mueller. *Gerald R. Ford* (Presidential Leaders). Breckenridge, CO: Twenty-First Century Books, 2007.

Woog, Adam. *The 1970s* (American History by Decade). Farmington Hills, MI: KidHaven Press, 2007.

WEB SITES

Gerald R. Ford Library and Museum

www.ford.utexas.edu/

Home page of the Gerald R. Ford Presidential Library and Museum. A great amount of content, plus many useful links.

President Gerald R. Ford

www.whitehouse.gov/kids/presidents/geraldford.html

The official White House for Kids page for President Ford.

Richard Nixon

www.historyplace.com/unitedstates/impeachments/nixon.htm

The History Place page about President Nixon's involvement in Watergate, and his eventual impeachment and resignation.

BIBLIOGRAPHY

Black, Conrad. *Richard M. Nixon: A Life in Full*. New York: PublicAffairs, 2007.

Boy Scouts of America National Council. "Scouts Mourn First Eagle Scout President." http://www.bsalegal.org/bsa-legal-blawg-200 .asp?i=79. December 27, 2006.

Brinkley, Douglas. *Gerald R. Ford*. New York: Henry Holt and Company, 2007.

Cannon, James. *Time and Chance: Gerald Ford's Appointment With History*. New York: HarperCollins, 1994.

DeFrank, Thomas M. *Write It When I'm Gone: Remarkable Off-the-Record Conversations with Gerald R. Ford*. New York: Putnam Adult, 2007.

Ford, Betty (with Chris Chase). *The Times of My Life*. New York: Harper & Row, 1978.

Ford, Gerald R. *A Time to Heal: The Autobiography of Gerald R. Ford*. New York: Harper & Row, 1979.

Microsoft Encarta 2008 Edition. "The United States Constitution."

Mieczkowski, Yanek. *Gerald Ford and the Challenges of the 1970s*. Lexington: The University of Kentucky Press, 2005.

Schulman, Bruce J. *The Seventies: The Great Shift in American Culture, Society, and Politics*. New York: The Free Press, 2001.

Shirer, William L. *The Rise and Fall of the Third Reich: A History of Nazi Germany*. New York: Simon and Schuster, 1960.

ter Horst, J. F. *Gerald Ford and the Future of the Presidency*. New York: The Third Press, 1974.

Waldman, Michael. *My Fellow Americans: The Most Important Speeches of America's Presidents, from George Washington to George W. Bush*. Naperville, IL: Sourcebooks MediaFusion, 2003.

Witcover, Jules. *Very Strange Bedfellows: The Short and Unhappy Marriage of Richard Nixon and Spiro Agnew*. New York: PublicAffairs, 2007.

Woodward, Bob. *Shadow: The Presidents and the Legacy of Watergate*. New York: Simon & Schuster, 1999.

INDEX

Pages in **boldface** are illustrations.

INDEX

ABOUT THE AUTHOR

Wil Mara is the author of more than a hundred books, including many reference titles for young readers. More information about his work, including a complete bibliography, can be found at www.wilmara.com.